Stories OF 20 MIGHTY MUSLIM HEROES

Heroes who help us believe in ourselves to make a difference

TAMARA HAQUE

ILLUSTRATED BY
GHADA EZZAT • SOUNDOS REZIG
TRISHA BOSE

National Library of Australia
Prepublication Data Service entry

Paperback ISBN: 978-0-6450774-0-7

Olive Tree Books

Second Edition

www.tamarahaque.com.au

Introduction

If you are Muslim you might find it difficult to find heroes you can relate to, but that shouldn't be the case. Did you know that the first nurse was Muslim? Did you know that the Father of Early Modern Medicine was Muslim? The oldest running university was founded by a Muslim woman. The man who travelled to nearly forty countries in the 14th century was Muslim. The Queen who spent over a billion dollars for the comfort of pilgrims was Muslim. The Bengali woman who advocated for girls' education was Muslim. The Father of Algebra was also a Muslim!

These are just some examples of thousands of Muslim heroes who helped to change the world over the centuries. This book hopes to inspire you with the stories of twenty such Muslim heroes. Travel back to a time where women and the poor did not have rights and read about the beautiful changes that Islam brought to people's lives. Read about the heroes during the Islamic Golden Age who made outstanding contributions to Science, Arts and Education. Learn about inspirational women who never backed down and left their mark in this world. Be inspired by people who were curious about the world until the day they died.

They were Muslims who believed in the beautiful teachings of Islam and also did great things for the world at the same time. Their faith helped them achieve their dreams and greatness. They were Muslims and they were heroes.

You are also a hero. Don't ever doubt yourself. Always keep your heart open.

Notes

- All dates are according to the Gregorian calendar.
- ﷺ Symbol for Sallalahu alaihi wa sallam (Peace and blessings be upon him). This salutation is used for Prophet Muhammad.
- ؓ Symbol for Radhiallahu 'anhu ('anha for female) (May God be pleased with him/her). This salutation is used for all of the companions of Prophet Muhammad ﷺ.
- All non-English words are listed in the glossary.
- A timeline has been created to show when each hero lived in history. See pages 8–9.
- All places mentioned in the book can be found on the illustrated map on pages 10–11.

The stories of the Prophet's companions have been reviewed by Ribaat Institute for authenticity.

Acknowledgements

This book is dedicated to Baba, Ma, my sister Monica, and my husband Shawqui, the four pillars of my life.

A special dedication to two little cuties, Manha and Jabir.

I would like to express my gratitude to Adiba for being my biggest cheerleader and your artistic input, Jessica for your encouragement, and Alina for reading the stories to your daughter.

I have a massive appreciation for my illustrators Ghada Ezzat, Soundos Rezig and Trisha Bose for bringing this book to life and making it look better than I ever imagined.

I'd also like to thank Penny Esterley for being my beta reader and giving me a much needed moral boost, and my editor Rose Barlow for her thorough job in making this book readable. And a huge thanks to Ellen Kokontis for creating the cover and book design of my dreams.

Alhamdulillah (Praise be to God) for all His blessings.

"The good deed and the bad deed are not equal. Return evil with good, and the person who was your enemy becomes like an intimate friend." (Holy Quran 41:34)

Contents

Muslim Heroes Timeline

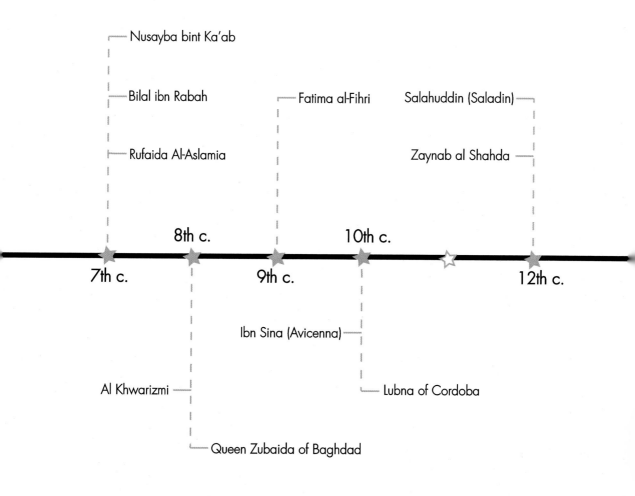

Nusayba bint Ka'ab

Bilal ibn Rabah

Rufaida Al-Aslamia

Fatima al-Fihri

Salahuddin (Saladin)

Zaynab al Shahda

8th c.

10th c.

7th c.

9th c.

12th c.

Ibn Sina (Avicenna)

Al Khwarizmi

Lubna of Cordoba

Queen Zubaida of Baghdad

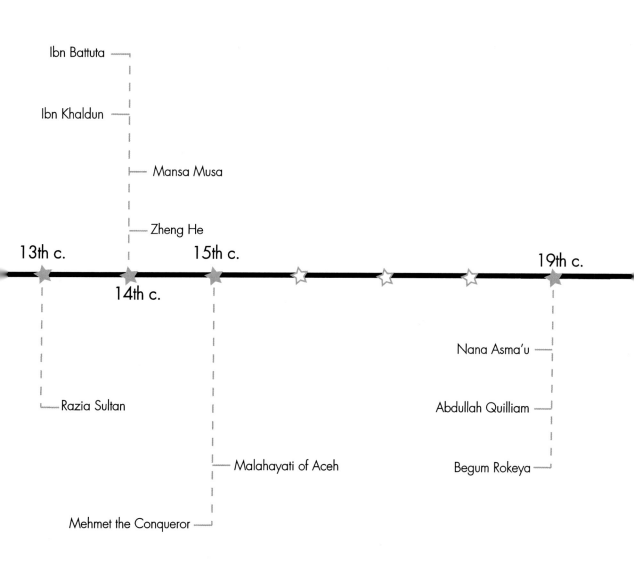

Ibn Battuta

Ibn Khaldun

Mansa Musa

Zheng He

13th c.   15th c.   19th c.

14th c.

Razia Sultan

Nana Asma'u

Abdullah Quilliam

Malahayati of Aceh

Begum Rokeya

Mehmet the Conqueror

• Liverpool

Europe

GOLDEN HORDE

Constantinople

PERSIA

Al-Rayy

Hamadan

Baghdad

ANDALUSIA

•Cordoba

Tunis

Damascus

•Fez

IRAQ

Acre

PALESTINE

Jerusalem

Isfahan

ALGERIA

EGYPT

Medina

Mecca

SAUDI
ARABIA

MALI

NIGERIA

Africa

ETHIOPIA
(ABYSSINIA)

SOMALIA

TANZANIA

WHERE WERE OUR HEROES?

A Map of Every Place in the Book

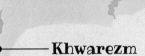

Khwarezm

Bukhara

Asia

Delhi

Bengal

Yunnan

BAHRAIN

Calicut

CEYLON

ACEH

Malacca Straits

MALDIVES

SUMATRA

JAVA

Soundos Rezig

Nusayba bint Ka'ab

First Muslim Female Warrior
7th Century

Do you know the story of Nusayba bint Ka'ab?
She was a fearless heroine who defended Prophet Muhammad during a battle even when she was gravely injured.

Before Islam, women in Arabia had very few human rights. Female babies were buried alive and women were sold as property. Islam gave a voice to women and gave them rights women did not have before.

Nusayba was a Muslim woman from Medina. She and many other women looked after the injured during the Battle of Uhud. The Muslims were on their road to victory, but overconfidence led to huge losses. Soldiers guarding the mountains surrendered their posts, and the Meccan army took this opportunity to attack them from behind. Many important Muslims, including the Prophet's Uncle Hamza, were killed.

A fierce battle followed and Prophet Muhammad was injured. Seeing this, Nusayba rushed to the battleground with her sword and bow to defend Prophet Muhammad, acting as a human shield. She cared more about the Prophet's life than her own. Prophet Muhammad later said, "Wherever I turned, to the left or the right, I saw her fighting for me." Such awesome courage!

Nusayba received twelve wounds during this battle. However, it didn't stop her from participating in future battles. She continued to take part even when she was sixty years old. She fought alongside men and women with her spear and sword. She was unstoppable even when she was wounded .

She and her family were very dear to the Prophet . Once, Nusayba asked the Prophet why most of the verses revealed so far in the Quran address only men . God then revealed the following verse in the Holy Quran:

"Muslim men and Muslim women, believing men and believing women, obedient men and obedient women, truthful men and truthful women, patient men and patient women, humble men and humble women, charitable men and charitable women, fasting men and fasting women, men who guard their chastity and women who guard, men who remember Allah frequently and women who remember—Allah has prepared for them a pardon, and an immense reward. [Holy Quran 33:35]

Nusayba's story is a story of hope for all Muslim girls given at a time when girls had no say. Nusayba was one of many women who played a big part in shaping the Muslim community. She was no longer oppressed. She was a strong Muslim woman who did not compromise on her faith or her life's purpose. She remains an example for everyone that Islam did not come to oppress women but give them their due rights.

Bilal ibn Rabah ﷺ

First Black Muslim and Muezzin
7th Century

We hear of racism existing around us. Some of us, sadly, may have even experienced it. Racism is never acceptable. People who think it is okay to hate others because of their colour come from ignorance.

Prophet Muhammad ﷺ preached that everyone was equal irrespective of colour. Our hero, Bilal ibn Rabah ﷺ, is proof of his teachings. Bilal ibn Rabah was an Ethiopian slave born in the late 6th century to slave parents in Mecca. He was one of the early converts to Islam. He remains a hero for every Muslim and those fighting against racism.

Bilal's father was a black Arab slave. However, his mother was a princess in Ethiopia who was captured and taken as a slave after a battle. As a result, Bilal, was born into slavery.

When Bilal's owner learned that Bilal had become Muslim, the owner began to torture Bilal so that he would give up his faith. The torture was so horrific; he placed heavy rocks on Bilal's chest, but Bilal said he would never give up on God. His faith in God was extremely firm. The torture continued and he was nearly killed. But then Abu Bakr , Prophet Muhammad's ﷺ very close friend, bought Bilal from the owner and set him free. Abu Bakr cared for him like his own brother and brought him back to good health. After recovering, Bilal was taken to Prophet Muhammad ﷺ, and Bilal remained his loyal companion until the end of the Prophet's life.

Prophet Muhammad ﷺ and the small Muslim community migrated to Medina because of the endless torture. Bilal was known for his beautiful voice. He would often recite poetry that people loved listening to. After migrating, Prophet Muhammad ﷺ requested Bilal to call the adhan, which is the Islamic call to prayer you hear from mosques. He went down in history as the first Muezzin. Bilal would call the prayer from the mosque and also through the streets of Medina. When the Muslims conquered Mecca, Bilal was given the honour to call the adhan from the Kaaba's top.

Bilal fought in battles beside the Prophet ﷺ and would carry his spear. He was recognized for his bravery, and Prophet Muhammad ﷺ loved him dearly. After the Prophet's death, Bilal moved to Damascus to continue spreading the message of Islam.

Bilal was seen as an equal. It did not matter what colour he was or that he used to be a slave. All that mattered was that he was a good human being and a good Muslim. Islam teaches us to never look down on someone because of their colour. Prophet Muhammad ﷺ said, "There is no superiority of an Arab over a non-Arab, or of a non-Arab over an Arab, and no superiority of a white person over a black person or of a black person over a white person, except in goodness and virtue."

Ghada Ezzat

Rufaida Al-Aslamia ﷺ

First Muslim Nurse and Female Surgeon
7th Century

You know of Florence Nightingale, the Mother of Modern Nursing, but there was someone many centuries before her who nursed soldiers during battles. She is our hero, Rufaida Al-Aslamia ﷺ, who lived during the time of the Prophet Muhammad ﷺ and is said to be the first female nurse and surgeon.

Rufaida was curious about the human body. Her father, who was a healer, taught her about it from a very young age. She learned how to take care of the sick and techniques on how to heal the wounded. Rufaida was so dedicated to learning about the human body and healing people that she became one of the most sought after healers in the community.

Her skills became critical during battles. With Prophet Muhammad's ﷺ permission, she set up tents along with female volunteers and treated the wounded . Rufaida was the one who trained these volunteers . Prophet Muhammad ﷺ trusted her abilities so much that there were many wounded soldiers he requested to only be taken to her tent for treatment . Not only did she nurse them, but she also performed surgery to save lives. It didn't matter how scary the battles were or how hot the weather was, Rufaida and the volunteers persisted in saving as many lives as they could.

But Rufaida's contribution was not only limited to battles. Our noble hero also designed the first ever documented mobile care units that could be moved from town to town to treat people . We know we are supposed to regularly wash our hands to get rid of germs. Well, Rufaida advocated washing hands and other hygiene practices way back then to prevent many diseases. She would walk from town to town, advising people to keep clean.

Rufaida developed new traditions and rules for better nursing, many of which you would find in modern nursing. Rufaida also wanted to give back to her people in other ways. She spent her time looking after the sick, orphans and the poor. She also taught others to become nurses and healers in their communities.

She was a kind, patient and committed woman who wanted to help as many people as she could. Today, she is still remembered by the RCSI Medical University in Bahrain, who awards the best nursing student with the Rufaida Al-Aslamia prize every year!

Rufaida is another example of a Muslim woman from the time of Prophet Muhammad ﷺ, who followed a path that may be surprising to many people today. She is one of the thousands of early Muslim women who were strong Muslims and followed their dreams and helped the world become a better place.

Ghada Ezzat

Al Khwarizmi

The Father of Modern Algebra
8th Century

Some of us love Math in school, and some of us hate it. It becomes even more complicated when letters get involved, and you have to solve equations! If you haven't guessed already, we are talking about algebra. Perhaps you haven't started it in school yet, but you will soon!

Our hero, Al Khwarizmi, is the one who developed the modern version of this complex subject to solve real-life problems. Algebra may seem hard, but it has made life much easier by enabling us to solve math problems much more quickly.

Al Khwarizmi was born in the late 8th century in Khwarezm. He was a scholar at the *House of Wisdom* in Baghdad. The House of Wisdom was a centre for studying sciences, including mathematics, medicine and astronomy. Al Khwarizmi wanted to make life easier. He wanted to figure out how to solve money issues, inheritance and engineering decisions quickly. This led to him write the very first algebra book. We get the word *algebra* from the title of his book *Kitab fi hisab al-jabr wa'l-muqabala* (this is the shortened title meaning Book on Calculation by Completion and Balancing). He wrote this book during his time in the House of Wisdom.

Al Khwarizmi studied various Greek and Hindu scholars and translated their works into Arabic. The numbers 1-9 and 0 were brought to the Islamic and Western world by Al Khwarizmi. The Arabs adopted the Arabic numerals and Latin translations of his work in the 12th century brought the numbers to the Western world. These numbers replaced the Roman numerals (V, VI, X, etc.). Al Khwarizmi also wrote a geography book; he helped construct a world map, and he contributed to a project to calculate the Earth's circumference. Did you know that the word *algorithm* comes from the Latin version of his name,

Al Khwarizmi? Wow! All these contributions just by one man, who changed the way we see Mathematics! Mathematics and algebra may seem hard but remember that we would not have had computers, planes, or even reached the moon without these important inventions! So, thank you, Al Khwarizmi, for paving the way for such wonders in our world!

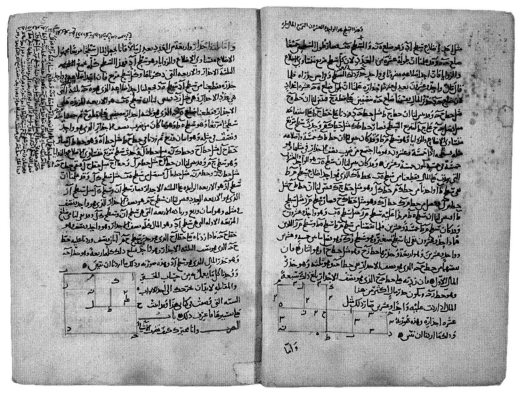

The Book on Calculation by Completion and Balancing
Mario Biondi writer, CC BY-SA 4.0 via Wikimedia Commons

Queen Zubaida of Baghdad

The Heart of Pilgrims
8th Century

Do you know the stories of Sindbad the Sailor, Ali Baba and the forty thieves, and Aladdin from The *Arabian Nights: Tales from a Thousand and One Nights*? You'll be surprised to know that this book was inspired by our hero in this chapter, Queen Zubaida and her husband Harun al-Rashid, the 8th century *Abbasid Caliph*.

Zubaida was an intelligent lady of immense beauty who lived in Baghdad. She learned the *Holy Quran,* studied Arabic literature and Islamic Studies. She married the Caliph Harun al-Rashid in 782 AD. Their empire's growth and developments in trade and technology meant that the empire became very wealthy. She invited many scientists, poets, and other intellectuals to Baghdad to make Baghdad a learning centre. According to stories, Zubaida's palace sounded like a beehive because of the Quran recitation day and night by Palace maids. She was also a deeply religious woman. She and her husband Harun went for *Hajj* many times and sometimes made the entire journey from Baghdad to Mecca on foot! The route was around 1,400km (900 miles) in length. That's like walking across 14,000 football pitches!

During this pilgrimage, Zubaida saw that many pilgrims were struggling to get water on Mecca's barren roads. This broke Zubaida's heart, and she ordered a canal to be built so that pilgrims would have access to water on the way. This was an extremely expensive project as it is difficult to access water in deserts and barren mountains, but Zubaida did not care about the cost. After a few years of construction, the canal was finally completed. It was called the "Zubaida Canal." Zubaida also built many free accommodations, wells, police posts, pools and mosques along the Baghdad–Mecca route.

Remains of the Zubaida Trail
Tahir mq, CC BY-SA 4.0 via Wikimedia Commons

The trail comprised several water wells that were perfectly designed, reflecting the brilliant Islamic engineering skills used. Pilgrims could rest, exchange ideas and meet people of different backgrounds and cultures, making the route come alive. It is said that in today's currency, the constructions would have cost billions of dollars! This route became known as the "Zubaida Trail." The trail served travellers for over 1,000 years until people started traveling by plane.

She was called *Al Saiyada Zubaida* (Lady Zubaida) because of her big heart, religiosity and helpful nature. She demonstrates to us all that money is not just for buying expensive things. We can help others and do good with our wealth because this is a gift from God.

Fatima al-Fihri

Founder of the Oldest Running University
9th Century

If anyone tells you that girls shouldn't have an education, tell them the story of Fatima al-Fihri. Not only was Fatima a woman, but she founded a university over 1,000 years ago that is still running today. In fact, it is older than Oxford and Cambridge!

Fatima al-Fihri was a Tunisian Muslim woman whose family settled in Fez, Morocco, in the 9th century. Her father ensured she and her sister were educated. They were also deeply religious. When her wealthy father and husband died, Fatima decided to use her inheritance to build a much-needed learning institution for her city. She called it *al-Qarawiyyin Mosque and University*, after her hometown. This university was built in 859 AD–more than 200 years before Oxford! The library is also considered the oldest library globally, and it had more than 4,000 books and manuscripts, which was an enormous amount for the time.

Fatima encouraged education for both boys and girls, and people from all over the world came to study at the university. In fact, one of our Muslim heroes in this book, Ibn Khaldoun, was a graduate of al-Qarawiyyin. Al-Qarawiyyin became famous as a place for debates on religious, academic and even political topics. Fatima's university established the university system as we know it today.

Interestingly, Fatima became a university student herself, and her degree, which was carved on a wooden board can be found displayed in the library today. With an unquenchable thirst for knowledge, Fatima continued attending lectures until her old age.

Not only was Fatima an advocate for education, but she was actively involved in helping all those around her. She donated a lot to charity. She was called 'The Mother of Boys' because of all the children she took under her wing to provide education and care.

Fatima was a legendary woman who ensured world-class education opportunities for both men and women, and no man questioned her intelligence or authority. She is a reminder that girls can also be highly educated and that education is not limited to boys. Her thirst for knowledge teaches us that one must remain curious about the world because there is always something new to learn.

Al-Qarawiyyin University, Abdel Hassouni, CC BY-SA 4.0 via Wikimedia Commons ▶

Ibn Sina (Avicenna)

Father of Early Modern Medicine
10ᵗʰ Century

We know Newton, Galileo and Einstein, but do you know who is called the Father of Early Modern Medicine? He is Ibn Sina (Avicenna in the West), and he was a polymath. A polymath is a person who has deep knowledge of a range of subjects. He was a scientist, physician, astronomer, mathematician, poet and philosopher. Phew! What an impressive resume! Ibn Sina is the most important scientific figure of the Islamic Golden Age.

He was the author of possibly over 450 books – enough to fill a small library! His most famous books are *The Canon of Medicine* (the *Qanun*) and *The Book of Healing*. The *Qanun* forever changed how we understood the human body. It remained the standard medical textbook in Islamic and European universities for 600 years after Ibn Sina's death. In fact, he was the first to study the antiseptic nature of alcohol. Antiseptics help in preventing infections. Alcohol is a very common antiseptic today.

Ibn Sina was born in Persia in 980 AD and became a Quran *Hafiz* at ten years old. He immersed himself in the study of medicine at sixteen years old and became a physician by the age of eighteen. At eighteen, he served as a physician for the *Sultan of Bukhara, Nuh II*. He cured the Sultan of an illness that baffled all the renowned physicians. The Sultan rewarded Ibn Sina by giving him access to the royal library. There he continued his research and read many rare manuscripts.

Ibn Sina set up a medical practice in *Al Rayy*. He would treat his poor patients for free. He also wrote around thirty books during his time there. He then moved to *Hamadan* and cured the ruler, *Emir Shams al-Dawlah*, of severe illness. The Emir, grateful and impressed, then appointed Ibn Sina as his physician and *Grand Vizier*.

He moved from Hamadan to *Isfahan* and finished his epic writings. He spent his final few years serving Isfahan's ruler *Emir Ala al-Dawlah*. Ibn Sina was around 57 years old when he died.

Ibn Sina was extremely curious about the soul and its connection to the body. He wrote that our souls are created with the body, and the body is used as a tool. The habits we form and the knowledge we gain contribute to the differences between souls. The soul continues to exist when we die with all the characteristics developed during our lives. He based his logic and assumptions on the teachings of the Holy Quran.

Another of Ibn Sina's impressive accomplishments was translating many Ancient Greek texts into Arabic. These texts advanced learning in the Islamic world and helped the Western world develop their understandings of Science and Philosophy centuries later.

Ibn Sina was a genius always in search of knowledge. He is a great Muslim hero who teaches us we always have to be on the path of knowledge to learn more about ourselves, about God and the world around us.

Trisha Bose

Lubna of Cordoba

The Library Queen
10th Century

This is the story of a woman who became one of the most important women of her time. She went from being a slave to being in charge of the royal library. She had many other accomplishments as well. This story is of Lubna of Cordoba.

Lubna lived in the 10th century AD and was raised in Cordoba, Spain. She was born a Spanish slave girl, but she became famous in the *Andalusian* court for her wide knowledge of language and grammar. She became the secretary and scribe of the *Caliph Al-Hakam II* and was in charge of the Royal Library of Cordoba. In a court full of men, this was a spectacular achievement.

Lubna collected books, plays, manuscripts and other writings for the library. She travelled to many cities and countries across North Africa and the Middle East searching for rare books. She was the driving force behind creating the famous library of *Medina Azahara* (Andalusian palace-city), which held over 500,000 books and manuscripts.

Not only did she collect books, but Lubna had the important task of copying and translating difficult texts from Greek to Arabic. This was an impressive achievement for anyone but even more so because of her difficult beginnings.

Lubna was also a prominent mathematician of her time. She could solve complex mathematical problems that others struggled with.

Lubna's other talent was poetry. She wrote many poems about life in the palace and her life in particular. Lubna taught local children during her free time, preparing the next generation of intellectuals.

It is said Lubna was one of several hundred female intellectuals in Andalusia at the time. This shows the importance of knowledge for both men and women in Andalusia and that women could also become important intellectual members of society.

Lubna's story is a story of talent, hard work and challenging society's expectations. It doesn't matter whether we are born poor or underprivileged. We can change our destiny through hard work and having even just one person believe in us.

Trisha Bose

Salahuddin (Saladin)

Great Warrior of Islam
12th Century

Salahuddin (Saladin in the West) was a famous ruler, fierce warrior and one of the greatest Muslim heroes. He was also the leader who recaptured Jerusalem in the Crusades, bringing it under Muslim rule for the next 750 years.

Salahuddin was born as Yusuf ibn Ayyub. He was of Kurdish background, and his family moved to Aleppo after his birth in the mid-12th century. Interestingly, Salahuddin was more concerned with studying Islam than in military training when growing up.

Salahuddin began his military career at 14 years old when he worked with his uncle, who held a high military post in Egypt. After a few battles, he became the military leader and was also appointed adviser to the *Sultan* in Egypt. After the death of the Sultan and ongoing conflict, Salahuddin led his army to claim the throne, and he became the Sultan of Egypt. Salahuddin wanted to unite the Muslim world. After the death of the Sultan of Damascus, Salahuddin led his army to Damascus and claimed the Sultan's position. His mission of uniting the Muslim world continued. He conquered lands between Egypt and Syria.

Most importantly, Salahuddin wanted to free largely Muslim areas from Crusaders and bring back Jerusalem to Muslim rule. Crusaders were European soldiers who started and fought wars to keep Holy Land under Christian rule, including Jerusalem. Crusaders captured Jerusalem in the First Crusade in 1099.

At the Battle of Hattin in 1187, Salahuddin and his army nearly destroyed the Crusader forces. This was the defining moment of the Crusades, and Jerusalem fell into Muslim hands. When the Crusaders overtook Jerusalem in the First Crusade, there was a bloody massacre of Muslim and Jewish residents. However, when Salahuddin entered Jerusalem, he surprised the crusaders by allowing many to go free or live in Jerusalem in harmony with the Muslims and Jews.

Salahuddin was a religious, honourable, generous man and leader. When Richard the Lion Heart (King of England) fell ill during his battles against Salahuddin, Salahuddin sent him ice and healing fruits. When his horse was killed, Salahuddin gifted him horses so the king wouldn't be at a disadvantage. Richard the Lion Heart and the Crusaders eventually captured the city of Acre; however, Salahuddin could keep the keys of Jerusalem through a peace-deal.

Salahuddin gave away most of his wealth for good causes and never missed a prayer. He died being remembered as one of the greatest heroes in the Muslim world and a just warrior in the European world.

Ghada Ezzat

zaynab al Shahda

Look around your home and see whether you have any beautifully written *dua's* or Quran verses framed. Do you see any? Those are the magnificence of calligraphy. Calligraphy is the art of beautiful handwriting. Our next hero was a master of calligraphy.

Zaynab al Shahda was born in Baghdad in the 12th century. Her father encouraged her education in Islamic Law, Quran, science and calligraphy.

Zaynab became a famous calligrapher and was appointed by the Caliph to use her art in the palace. She was also well known for her work in Islamic law and *hadith* and became one of the Caliph teachers. Zaynab was known for her intelligence, and students came from all over to learn from her. She was also known for her witty replies to questions and comments from people.

Zaynab spent her free time studying science and literature and also improving her calligraphy techniques. Zaynab's art was not only used in the palace but in several books and manuscripts. She passed away in Baghdad at nearly 100 years old.

Parents must encourage their children's talents and enable them to gain a wonderful education. Zaynab al Shahda was proof that women can excel in a range of areas and be an excellent teacher to both girls and boys.

Soundos Rezig

Trisha Bose

Razia Sultan

First and Only Muslim Female Ruler
of Delhi Sultanate
13th Century

There are very few women rulers we hear of from the past; of these few, *Queen Elizabeth I* is probably the most famous. Our next hero is a ruler from the Indian subcontinent who fought in battles on the front line and predated Elizabeth by at least three centuries.

Razia was the first and only female ruler of the Sultanate of Delhi from 1236 – 1240. She was the only daughter of *Sultan Iltutmish*, and along with his sons, he ensured Razia was also educated and trained in archery and administration.

Razia was in charge of the Delhi Sultanate in 1232 whilst her father was away on a campaign. Her abilities impressed her father and announced Razia to be his heir after his death. This was a surprise as women were generally not successors in the Muslim or even Christian world at the time. After her father's death, schemers planned to keep her from the throne, and a new Sultan was appointed. However, the Sultan proved to be highly incompetent, and Razia finally started her rule in 1236.

Razia didn't grow up around many women, so she wasn't very familiar with the rules and behaviours royal women had to follow. She voiced her opinions, was bold, and even wore neutral outfits raising many eyebrows in court.

Razia refused to be addressed as 'Sultana', which means 'wife of Sultan'. She insisted on being called Sultan instead because she was indeed the Sultan - the Ruler. During her rule, Razia even mounted an elephant as the chief of her army on the battlefield. Soldiers couldn't tell that they were fighting a woman! She fought on the forefront and won many battles. She founded many schools and libraries where she encouraged Islamic teachings as well as science, literature and philosophy from different religions.

Razia Sultan had coins printed with her name on them and called herself the 'Queen of the times'. She expanded her territories and gained many admirers and supporters in the Sultanate.

However, jealousy ensued amongst the nobles, and Razia Sultan ultimately met an unhappy ending. Her court and her siblings betrayed her, and she was eventually killed. Nonetheless, she is still remembered for her bravery at battles, her great rule, and her support for learning.

Many stories, songs and poems have been written about her bravery and confidence. She is the warrior princess little girls dream of being.

Ibn Battuta

The Great Explorer
14th Century

Do you like to travel and discover new places and cultures? Then you will love the story of our next hero. This is the story of Ibn Battuta, who started traveling by going to Mecca for *Hajj* and then travelled for the next 30 years, mostly around the Islamic world. He travelled to around forty countries!

Ibn Battuta was a Muslim legal scholar born in Morocco in the early 14th century. During this time, Islamic civilisation stretched from the Middle East to West Africa, to India and Southeast Asia. This was called the *Dar al-Islam* (House of Islam).

Ibn Battuta set out for Hajj at 20 years old, and on completion of Hajj, he continued traveling because he enjoyed seeing new places and cultures. He had spent time in Egypt and Damascus on his way to Mecca. While in Egypt, Ibn Battuta visited a saint, and he had a dream of an enormous bird that would carry him towards the East, leaving him there. The saint interpreted that Ibn Battuta would travel to India and stay there for a long time. Ibn Battuta did not forget this dream.

After travelling through Iraq and Persia, Ibn Battuta went back to Mecca to do Hajj again and studied Law for around a year. His adventures then took him down the red sea to Yemen and across to East Africa. He explored Ethiopia, Somalia, Tanzania and other beautiful places. Arabic wasn't their language, and Islam was still not the majority religion at the time, but Ibn Battuta would be warmly welcomed as a brother in Islam.

He then made his way to Anatolia, where he hoped to connect with a Turkish caravan and travel to India. According to Ibn Battuta, this country was one of the world's finest, and the men showed great respect for women. From here, he crossed the Black Sea and explored what was then known as 'The Golden Horde', part of Russia and Eastern Europe. This was part of the Mongol empire. From here, he travelled to Constantinople, which was still under *Christian Byzantine* rule.

After a four-month journey, Ibn Battuta finally made it to the Sultanate of Delhi, fulfilling the dream he had seen. He started to work for *Sultan Muhammad Tughluq* as a judge, but the Sultan was a very cruel man, even for the Middle Ages, and Ibn Battuta feared for his life. However, the Sultan made him an offer he couldn't refuse. The Sultan wanted him to be the ambassador to the Mongol court of China. This would be Ibn Battuta's opportunity to explore lands even further away (and be far away from the Sultan), so he said yes.

Unfortunately, misfortune fell on Ibn Battuta as he set out on this journey in style with at least 1,000 soldiers protecting the Mongol Emperor's gifts. They were robbed

Ghada Ezzat

many times. Ibn Battuta lost most of his belongings during a violent storm. He also lost many of the Emperor's gifts on the ship he was meant to sail on. He was left penniless. He feared the Sultan would kill him if he returned to Delhi, having failed his mission.

He decided to continue to China but on a much longer route via Ceylon and Maldives. The King of Ceylon had given him precious gems as a parting gift, but Ibn Battuta's bad luck continued and pirates attacked his ship. Again he was penniless.

Now though he was determined to continue to China alone. Ibn Battuta remembered Prophet Muhammad's ﷺ words, "Seek knowledge, even as far as China." While it doesn't mean that we have to go to China for knowledge, we must try to go wherever we can to gain wisdom. He travelled through Bengal, Sumatra and Java before finally landing in China.

The Rihla
Osama Shukir Muhammed Amin FRCP(Glasg), CC BY-SA 4.0 via Wikimedia Commons

From southern to possibly northern China, Ibn Battuta saw a large part of this great country. According to him, China was the safest country in the world. Having reached the far ends of the world, Ibn Battuta made his way back to Damascus.

In Damascus, he witnessed the effects of the *Black Death*. There were dead bodies everywhere, and communities had been wiped out. It was a very scary time for the world and much worse than what we have seen with the Coronavirus Pandemic in 2020. Ibn Battuta decided to continue to Mecca. Seeing even more death around him, he felt that he needed to head back home now and see his parents, family and friends.

On reaching Morocco, he learned that his mother had sadly passed away. He started feeling restless and decided to explore Andalusia, followed by Mali in Western Africa. When finally returning to Morocco for good, he was commanded by the Sultan to narrate his adventures to be written into a book, *The Rihla*. Many centuries later, this book was translated into different languages by European scholars, and the stories of his travels became famous.

Ibn Battuta died a few years later, leaving behind a thirst for adventure and a fascinating book on his travels. Every day can be an adventure for us so long as we remain curious about our surroundings, keeping an eye out for something new.

Ibn Khaldoun

Father of Social Sciences and Economics
14th Century

Ibn Khaldoun was one of the most important thinkers of the Middle Ages, who pioneered sociology and is also known as the Father of Economics. He was also a famous historian and wrote a great deal about Islam.

Ibn Khaldoun was born in Tunis, Africa, in the mid-14th century. His family members served important government posts, and he received his education in the Quran, Arabic Literature, Mathematics and Islamic Law. He studied at *al-Qarawiyyin* University, the oldest university that we have already learned about in Chapter 6! He also served in governmental positions in Africa and Andalusia. Unfortunately, he faced problems in politics, and he did not want to be involved any longer.

On returning to Africa, Ibn Khaldoun retreated to Algeria and began writing his most important book, *Muqaddimah* (Introduction), introducing his planned history of the world. He then returned to his hometown Tunis to finish his book. This book was not only important from a historical view but also for Social Sciences. He observed that when a society becomes a great civilisation; the greatness is followed by a period of decline. This is followed by a group of barbarians taking over who then become cultured and sophisticated by learning from the locals. This process is repeated again and again.

The book also talked about important and major concepts in Economics, over 300 years before Adam Smith came up with modern Economics.

After writing this very important book, he sailed to Egypt and spent his remaining years there. He became a teacher in Egypt and was made a chief judge and interpreter of Islamic law. Ibn Khaldoun also wrote his autobiography, which gave an insight into daily life in Muslim countries.

Ibn Khaldoun remains one of the most important thinkers of the Islamic Golden Age. His works paved the way for Europeans to develop these areas of study further.

Bust of Ibn Khaldoun, Reda Kerbouche, CC BY-SA 4.0 via Wikimedia Commons ▶

IBN KHALDOUN

Mansa Musa

The Richest Person in the World
14th Century

The superhero Black Panther, and the king of Wakanda, was supposed to be the richest Marvel Comics superhero—even richer than Iron Man. There is a real African king, however, who was possibly the richest person ever to live. He is our next hero, Mansa Musa. He had so much wealth that people say it cannot be counted. Let's find out more about this fascinating ruler.

Mansa Musa was the ruler of the Kingdom of Mali in West Africa in the early 14th century. His kingdom was one of the richest, spreading far beyond Mali, across West Africa.

Many have written about Musa, including two of our heroes Ibn Khaldun and Ibn Battuta. People realized the unbelievable wealth of Musa when he set out for Hajj in 1324.

Musa set out with over 50,000 of his people and servants. They carried thousands of kilograms in gold on camels and elephants. When Musa reached Egypt, he met the Sultan. Musa was asked to bend his knee in front of the Sultan, but he refused. He said that he could only do that for God. Musa was a deeply religious man. In Egypt, he and his caravan gave away so much gold that Egyptian gold's value collapsed. It took 12 years for the value of Egyptian gold to recover. News of his riches travelled to Europe. The Spanish created a map of West Africa, showing Mansa Musa sitting on his throne with a lot of gold. He became the symbol of enormous wealth.

However, Musa also used his wealth to do a lot of good. Every Friday during his pilgrimage, Musa would order the building of a mosque wherever he was. On his return, he brought scholars, engineers, traders from North Africa and Andalusia to develop Mali into an important cultural centre and place of learning. Timbuktu became a very famous city for Islamic learning and cultural capital. You may have heard of 'Timbuktu' being used to describe a place far away. Now you know where this city actually is!

Many of the mosques Musa built still exist today. Musa was not only a symbol of wealth. He was also a generously religious man who wanted to educate people and spread Islam's true teachings.

Mansa Musa in the Catalan Atlas, published in 1375.
Bibliothèque nationale de France, Public domain, via Wikimedia Commons ▶

aquest
mulli...
de si po...
rich el...
esta r...
qual s...

Zheng He

Chinese Muslim Explorer
14th century

We don't hear about many Muslims from China, so this story is exciting! Zheng He (birth name Ma He) was a Chinese Muslim explorer born in the late 14th century in the Yunnan province of China. Ma is the Chinese version of the name 'Muhammad', and he was born to a Muslim family. After Ma He's father and grandfather returned from *Hajj*, Ma asked many questions about the people, the journey and the places they visited. Sadly, Yunnan was attacked shortly after, and Ma was taken as a slave for one of the princes while still a child.

But Ma was a very hardworking boy, and he rose in rank amongst the slaves and servants. The Prince noticed his intelligence, and Ma soon became one of his most trusted advisors. When the Prince became Emperor, he renamed Ma to Zheng He, which remained his name till the end of his life. The Prince wanted to promote trade with other parts of the world and show the world the Chinese empire's power, so he appointed Zheng He as the Chief Envoy (commander-in-chief) of the missions known as the 'Western Oceans'.

Zheng He's first voyage consisted of over 200 ships and nearly 28,000 men. The fleet sailed through South East Asia and finally to Calicut on the southern coast of India. People were in awe of the massive fleet and the power of the Chinese empire. This voyage lasted two years.

Zheng He went on six more voyages after this, traveling across Sumatra, Java, Ceylon, the Maldives, Southern India, Bengal, Arabia, and East Africa. He is said to have travelled to over 25 countries. On his final voyage, Zheng He took a detour and performed Hajj in Mecca. The Chinese bought spices, traded other goods and established relationships with local traders and rulers. He brought back many interesting items, including animals such as camels!

Zheng He died during his journey home, and it remains a mystery whether he made it back to China.

Zheng He was a diplomatic man able to understand different cultures and treat them all respectfully. He realised his childhood dream of traveling despite having a very difficult childhood. Despite his enormous responsibilities, he still took the time to fulfil his religious obligations, including performing *Hajj*.

Ghada Ezzat

Malahayati of Aceh

First Female Admiral
15th Century

Keumalahayati, better known as Malahayati, was born in the 15th century in the *Aceh Sultanate*. She was the first female admiral of the navy in the world. Not only was she female but a Muslim too. Let's find out more about this courageous and admirable woman.

Malahayati was the daughter of Admiral Mahmud Syah of the Aceh Empire. After studying in an Islamic school, Malahayati continued her education at the Aceh Military Academy. She married her true love, but sadly he was killed during the war against Portuguese invaders. Determined to continue her husband's fight, Malahayati requested to form and lead a faction called *Inong Balee*, made up of Aceh's widows, to go into battle. This was an all-woman army. Yes, they were all women and they fought the Portuguese and Dutch, becoming one of the most feared fighting forces in the Sumatra!

The Sultan then formed a powerful navy and appointed Malahayati as his First Admiral. She fought two battles against the Dutch, defeated them, and fought a battle against the Portuguese army. Malahayati's powerful reputation led England to enter the Malacca Straits peacefully. Queen Elizabeth I sent a letter through her navy and Malahayati was in charge of making sure there was peace.

Malahayati was unfortunately killed in combat during a battle against the Portuguese, just like her husband. She was proud to have died defending her country and her faith. Malahayati was a heroic warrior who gave Aceh's widows a purpose. She was truly a force to be reckoned with.

Soundos Rezig

Mehmet the Conqueror

Conqueror of Constantinople
15th Century

"**O**ne day, Constantinople will be conquered. How wonderful and blessed are the leader of its conquest and his soldiers!" This was said by Prophet Muhammad ﷺ during his lifetime about the future conquest of Muslims of the centre of the Christian world. Many Muslim leaders tried to conquer Constantinople (modern-day Istanbul) to make this *hadith* a reality, but they failed until the great *Ottoman* Sultan, Mehmet II. This chapter is about his brilliance.

Sultan Fatih Mehmet II was born in 1432. After Mehmet's elder brother died, his father Murad II resigned from the throne and made Mehmet the new sultan at 12 years old. However because of disputes in territories that Mehmet was too young to handle, Murad II was forced to come back to the throne just two years later.

While Mehmet willingly gave the throne to his father, he felt humiliated. He spent his time learning and improving his military skills, getting ready for the day he would become the sultan again. His time came in 1451 after his father's death. Mehmet was very ambitious, and he wanted to prove himself by capturing Constantinople, where everyone else had failed. This would also mean the end of the Byzantine Empire. He spent the first year strengthening the Ottoman navy and signing peace treaties with neighbours to not interfere with his plans. In 1453 he set out for Constantinople with an army of possibly 200,000 soldiers and a navy of 320 warships.

The city was surrounded by land and sea, and the Siege of Constantinople began in early April 1453. Constantinople was bordered by tall, thick walls that no one had been able to breakthrough in centuries. Sultan Mehmet used a super cannon to fire the walls for weeks, which helped weaken them. Nobody had seen a cannon like this before. But they still could not cross the harbour which was blocked by a boom chain. Mehmet had the lighter warships heaved overland with a stroke of genius using wooden logs, bringing them even closer to defeating the Byzantines.

After a 57 day siege, Constantinople finally surrendered on May 29, 1453. Mehmet conquered Constantinople at the young age of 21 and called himself Mehmed the Conqueror. Mehmet wanted to make Constantinople the greatest city, and he had Turks from all over the empire, Greeks and Armenians settled in Constantinople. Many schools, buildings, mosques and centres were built. Constantinople became a social and economic centre, and it flourished with diverse faiths and cultures.

Painting of Mehmet the Conqueror
Fausto Zonaro, Public domain, via Wikimedia Commons

Mehmet was a very intelligent man who could speak Persian, Arabic and also ancient Greek and Latin. He loved poetry and the arts and built an enormous library. He was open-minded and had people from different faiths and backgrounds in his government. He died at the age of 49. Mehmet is remembered not only as one of the greatest Ottoman Sultans but one of the greatest Muslim leaders of all time.

Nana Asma'u

Nigerian Poet and Women's Education Leader
19ᵗʰ Century

Our next hero was a lovely princess in Western Africa. She championed education for girls and was a talented poet. Let's learn more about the inspirational Nana Asma'u.

Nana Asma'u was an Islamic scholar, poet, and educational leader in the 19th century. She was the daughter of Usman dan Fodio, the leader of the *Sokoto Caliphate*. This kingdom was one of the most powerful African kingdoms at the time.

Her early years were spent attaining a religious education from scholars within her family and her community. She also learned Science, Literature and eventually became fluent in six languages! Her family believed that gaining knowledge was a must, and it should also be shared.

Many girls in her community were married as young as ten years old, and their education stopped once they got married. Nana wanted to change this so in the 1830s, Nana created a group of female teachers called *yan-taru*, which means 'those who gather together; the sisterhood'. They called these teachers *jajis*. They travelled throughout the kingdom, teaching girls and boys, Muslim and non-Muslim, rich and poor. Their goal was to share knowledge with everyone. Each *jaji* was given a *malfa*, a balloon-shaped hat men usually wore over their turbans. People identified the *jajis* by these hats.

Nana was also an advisor to her brother when he became Caliph. Nana confidently debated with princes and scholars. She also translated lessons, poetry and meetings as she was fluent in six languages. She was a respected poet and wrote a large collection of poetry. She even used poetry for the lessons to make them more interesting.

Nana Asma'u's efforts made education accessible to all of the West African kingdom. She empowered women and girls and ensured both boys and girls got an education. She believed that girls should use their God-given talents. Nana is an inspirational leader for us all.

Soundos Rezig

Abdullah Quilliam

Founder of the First Mosque in Britain
19ᵗʰ Century

It is not common to hear of a white British Muslim, but our next hero will change that. He not only converted to Islam but founded the first mosque in England in 1889.

Abdullah Quilliam (birth name William Henry Quilliam) was born in Liverpool, England, in 1856. He was a lawyer, writer and activist. He converted to Islam at 31 years old after he visited Morocco. He loved the way Muslims treated each other, hearing the *adhan* and the teachings of Islam.

After his conversion, Quilliam purchased land with the Crown Prince of Afghanistan's help and set up the Liverpool Muslim Institute, the first mosque and Islamic centre in Britain. There was a lot of racism at that time in Britain. People of different colours or backgrounds would not mix with each other. But the mosque was special because Muslims from different backgrounds and races could pray together, just as Muslims do across the world, just as Prophet Muhammad ﷺ

prayed. Quilliam was also the *Sheikh* of this mosque.

Many British people converted because they were inspired by Quilliam preaching. This included professors, politicians and women. Quilliam wrote many books about Islam, educating people about Islam's beautiful teachings. He helped changed the negative views many people had about Islam.

Quilliam travelled through the Islamic world and was given much recognition for his efforts in educating people about Islam. Quilliam also protested against Muslims fighting Muslims in wars. He believed in peace.

While some of Quilliam's works were lost after his death, his legacy lives on as the Founder of the first British mosque and inspiring British Muslims decades later.

Most people will learn with surprise that there is a flourishing Moslem mission to the English people in existence in Liverpool, and that about twenty persons annually embrace the creed of the Koran. The president, or as he styles himself the sheik, of the Liverpool Moslems is an Englishman, Mr. W. H. Quilliam, who became converted to the tenets of Islam some years ago. He is a solicitor with a large practice and to his coreligionists is known as Abdullah Quilliam, Sheik ul Islam of the British Isles. The Moslems have a mosque in the West Derby Road where every Friday prayers are held and on Sunday evenings lectures are given. They have also an orphanage for destitute children known as the Medina Home, and no matter how much one may differ from their creed they must be awarded every credit for their sincerity and unobtrusive charity. The ceremonies that every now and then occur in the mosque recall the Arabian Nights.

The Sheik ul Islam is attired in magnificent oriental robes of crimson and blue, and he is usually supported by gorgeously-clad Indians, Turks, or negroes. All Orientals that visit Liverpool who are Mahomedans naturally visit the mosque, and the richness of the scene at times baffles description. Some time ago a wedding according to Islamitic rites was celebrated in the mosque, the bride being English. The ceremony was very simple and beautiful, and served to show that after all it was largely prejudice and ignorance that caused the antipathy between the Cross and the Crescent.

It is notable that the European has modified certain aspects of the primitive Mahomedan creed, which in certain of its prohibitory laws—especially respecting food —is much akin to Judaism. It is estimated that 14 per cent. of the human race are Mahomedans. In India King Edward has among his subjects no fewer than 45,000,000 Moslems, and the creed has made considerable progress among the African races as the invading European Powers know to their cost. Londoners recently had an opportunity of studying the Mahomedan in the case of the Indian soldiers who came here for the coronation.

Mr. T. F. Dale, the well-known writer on polo, deals with " Riding and Polo Ponies " in the book just published by Lawrence and Bullen. The book is more or less an " advocacy of the use and an appreciation of our native breeds of ponies in building up a race of riding ponies suitable for polo or military purposes." He believes firmly that it is possible to breed ponies to a type, and he joins issue with Captain Miller on one or two important points about native ponies.

THE LIVERPOOL MOSQUE
Moslem devotion led by the Sheik ul Islam

Begum Rokeya

19th century Muslim Feminist

Our final hero is a rebel who fought for girls' rights to education. She was a leader who helped underprivileged women. She was a brilliant Muslim woman who used irony to educate people on women's rights.

Begum Rokeya was born in Bengal in 1880. She was a writer, an educator and India's first Islamist-feminist. She was born before India became divided into India, Bangladesh and Pakistan.

Begum Rokeya's father insisted that she and her sister Karimunnesa only be educated in Arabic so they could recite the Quran and were not sent to school. Nevertheless, Rokeya's brothers secretly taught Rokeya and her sister Bengali and English as well.

At that time, most Bengali Muslim girls did not go to school and spent most of their time at home. Begum Rokeya realised women could only become who they truly are meant to be through education. She moved to Calcutta and set up a Muslim girls' school with less than ten students. It was difficult to get parents to agree to send their daughters to school. But Rokeya didn't give up. She went from Muslim family to family, encouraging them to send their girls to school, informing them of the benefits of educating their daughters. And she succeeded. The school taught many languages, Quran, mathematics, cooking, sewing, and other subjects. *Begum Rokeya Smriti Balika Vidyalaya* remains one of the most popular girls' schools in Calcutta today.

Rokeya also started the Islamic Women's Association. Through this association, poor women and women that needed help were given financial, educational and emotional support. She was also a popular writer on women's rights and wrote short stories and novels, including her famous Sultana's Dream. In this book, men and women's roles were reversed, where men were the ones who had to stay home and face a lot of discrimination from people. Her books were popular because of her humorous and rebellious writing.

Begum Rokeya lost her husband and two children early in life, which made people talk about her, but she did not listen to any of these rumours and continued to fight for women's rights and education. She was a feminist who believed in the rights given to women by Islam. She is an inspiration for Muslims and girls worldwide as we continue the fight for women's rights!

Public Domain via Wikimedia Commons ▶

Name Pronunciations

Abdullah Quilliam – Ab-dul-lah Kee-liam

Begum Rokeya – Beh-gum Roh-keh-ya

Bilal ibn Rabah – Bi-laal ib-n Ra-bah

Fatima al-Fihri – Fa-ti-ma al-Fih-ree

Ibn Battuta – Ib-n Buh-too-tah

Ibn Khaldoun – Ib-n Kh-al-doon

Al-Khwarizmi – Al Kh-wa-riz-mee

Ibn Sina – Ib-n See-na

Lubna of Cordoba – Lub-nah of Cor-dob-ah

Malahayati of Aceh – Ma-lah-ha-ya-tee of Ah-cheh

Mansa Musa – Mun-sah Moo-sah

Mehmet the Conqueror – Meh-met the Con-cuh-rur

Nana Asma'u – Nah-nah Us-muh-oo

Nusayba bint Ka'ab – Nu-sa-ee-ba bint Ka-ub

Queen Zubaida of Baghdad – Queen Zu-bay-dah of Ba-gh-daad

Razia Sultan – Rah-zee-ah Sul-taan

Rufaida Al-Aslamia – Ru-fa-ee-da Al-Us-laa-mia

Salahuddin – Suh-lah-hood-deen

Zaynab al Shahda – Zay-nub al-Shuh-dah

Zheng He – Chuh-ng Huh

Glossary

Abbasid

A dynasty of Muslim rulers who ruled the Islamic empire from the 8th to the 13th century.

Aceh Sultanate

A kingdom in Sumatra (present day Indonesia) from the 15th to 19th centuries.

Adhan

Islamic call for prayer recited from mosques.

Admiral

Commander of the seas (the navy).

Allah

The Arabic word for God.

Astronomy

Astronomy is the study of the universe including stars and planets.

Battle of Uhud

This was the second battle between the Muslims and the Pagans (idol worshippers) of Mecca.

Black Death

A deadly plague that spread across many parts of the world in the 14th century.

Byzantine

The Eastern Roman empire from the 4th to the 15th centuries. This was founded by Constantinople.

Caliph

A successor of the Prophet. They were the leaders of their empires.

Christian

Followers of Christianity. This is a monotheistic religion that follows Jesus's message.

Circumference

Distance around the outside of a circle.

Crusades

Wars fought by the European Christians against Muslims to control and capture holy lands such as Jerusalem.

Dua

A supplication or prayer made to God

Emir

A ruler, commander of an Islamic country or empire.

Grand Vizier

The chief officer of state of an Islamic empire. Like the Prime Minister.

Hadith

Sayings of Prophet Muhammad ﷺ.

Hafiz

Someone who memorises the entire Quran.

Hajj

The major pilgrimage that Muslims have to do to Makkah at least once in their life.

Holy Quran

The holy book of Muslims.

Islam

A religion that preaches believing in one God (monotheistic religion) and Prophet Muhammad ﷺ as the last messenger.

Islamic Golden Age

The period between the 8th century and 13th centuries when science, arts, culture, education flourished throughout the Islamic empire.

Jewish

Followers of the Judaism religion. This is a monotheistic religion that follows the teachings of Moses.

Kaaba

The Kaaba is the building at the centre of the holiest mosque in Mecca, The Sacred Mosque. Muslims face the Kaaba to perform their prayers. The Kaaba is believed by Muslims to first have been built by Abraham.

Mecca

Holiest city for Muslims, located in Saudi Arabia. This is where the Kaaba is located.

Medina

Second holiest city for Muslims, located in Saudi Arabia.

Mongol empire

Mongols were a group of tribes from Central Asia. They ruled a vast empire from the 13th to 14th centuries.

Muezzin

The person who calls the prayer (adhan) from the mosque.

Muslim

The believers of the religion Islam are called Muslim. There are around 1.8 billion Muslims in the world.

Ottoman

The Turkish empire from the 14th to early 20th century.

Prophet Muhammad ﷺ

He is the last Prophet and Messenger sent by God according to Islam. He preached the same message as Abraham, Moses and Jesus.

saint

A person said to be close to God.

scribe

A person who copies writing from a book or another source.

sheikh

An elder or a leader of a Muslim group.

sociology

The study of human societies.

sultan

A ruler of an Islamic empire.

Sultanate of Delhi

A Muslim Kingdom in Northern India from the 13th to 16th centuries.

Bibliography

About Abdullah Quilliam http://www.abdullahquilliam.org/about-abdullah-quilliam/

Bilal ibn Rabah The Mu'addhin, Abdul Basit Ahmad, Darus-Salam Publications. 2004

Crusaders, Rob Llyod Jones, Usborne Publishing Ltd. 2007

Hossain Y. *The Begum's Dream: Rokeya Sakhawat Hossain and the Broadening of Muslim Women's Aspirations in Bengal.* South Asia Research. 1992;12(1):1-19.

Ibn Sina A concise life, Edoardo Albert, Kube Publishing Ltd. 2013

Ibn Battuta The journey of a medieval Muslim, Edoardo Albert, Kube Publishing Ltd. 2019

Jewels of Muslim Calligraphy: Book Review of "Female Calligraphers: Past & Present, Hilal Kazan, Istanbul Büyüksehir Belediyesi Kültür Isleri Daire Baskanligi. 2010

Labana of Cordoba https://muslimheritage.com/womens-contribution-to-classical-islamic-civilisation-science-medicine-and-politics/

Meet the First Female Admiral in the Modern World. Not from the West. https://seasia.co/2018/05/14/meet-the-first-female-admiral-in-the-modern-world-not-from-the-west

Mehmed the Conqueror http://www.theottomans.org/english/campaigns_army/Mehmed-the-Conqueror.asp

Nusaybah Bint Ka'ab - The First Woman Warrior of Islam http://www.nuseibehfamily.net/articles/12-articles/66-nusaybah-bint-ka-ab-the-first-woman-warrior-of-islam

Poem by Naana Asmaa'u. The British Library. https://www.bl.uk/collection-items/naana-asmaau-poem

Rufaida Al-Aslamia - the first Muslim nurse https://saudigazette.com.sa/article/175811

The Arab Muslim Woman Who Brought Higher Education to the Entire World, https://www.girlboss.com/

About the Author

Tamara is a Bangladeshi-Australian who spent her childhood in Saudi Arabia. Her favourite authors as a child were Roald Dahl, Enid Blyton and Charles Dickens. These authors gave her many heroes to look up to, Matilda being her favourite.

Tamara loved her multicultural upbringing but didn't always find it easy to embrace her Muslim identity. Reading about Islam's rich history and its great heroes surely helped. She wanted to write this book because she wants to inspire children and adults alike to be proud of their Muslim identity.

When Tamara isn't writing, she is likely reading, sketching, discovering new places, new food, new cultures, or talking to her plants. She will also be your best friend if you introduce her to your puppy.

About the Illustrators

Trisha Bose

Trisha Bose is an artist, who lives in New Delhi, India. She paints to feed herself and her family of dogs. She likes said dogs, history, fantastical adventures, and very spicy food. When she gets some free time, she shops to restock her snack cabinet, and makes a lot of fan art. She prefers hills to beaches, and tea to coffee!
www.trishabose.com

Soundos Rezig

Soundos Rezig is a Toronto based illustrator. Canadian born and of Algerian descent, she didn't see much representation of Muslim and Women of Colour in the animation and illustration world when growing up. Through her illustrations, Soundos highlights and shares the cultural diversity of her African and Muslim roots. Her aim is for children to see their image reflected in her artistic vision that is inclusive of everyone.
Instagram: @sounbosie

Ghada Ezzat

Ghada Ezzat is a freelance illustrator who loves working on children's books, card games and portraits. Ghada also owns an online gift shop. When Ghada isn't working, she loves doing crafts with her son Younis. She also loves reading, taking photos of everyday life and cooking delicious meals that her son and husband will devour.
Facebook: Ghada Ezzat Art

Endnotes

i Hadith (Bukhari, Al-Adab al-Mufrad:1129)

ii Hadith (Ibn al-Athir, Usd al Ghaba Fi Ma'rifat Al Sahaba: 6925)

iii Hadith (Bukhari, Al-Adab al-Mufrad:1129)

iv Rufaida Al-Aslamia - the first Muslim nurse https://saudigazette.com.sa/article/175811

v Hadith (Masnud of Imam Ahmad ibn Hanbal: 19774)

vi Al-Isaabah fi Tameezis-Sahaabah, ibn Hajar al-Asqalaani

vii Tafsir, al-Qurtubi, Hadith reported by Tirmidhi.

viii Hadith (Musnad Ahmad, Al Hakim, al Jami' al Saghir by Al-Suyuti)

Reviews are important to help books get discovered. They help readers, parents and teachers decide whether this book is for them.

Fun fact: Sales of the Mighty Muslim Heroes series increased 100% with an increase in reviews!

We would love your review if you enjoyed Stories of 20 More Mighty Muslim Heroes! Please scan the barcode below to leave a review on our website or on Amazon.

Alternatively, you could leave a review on Goodreads.com or your favourite online bookstore.

Find fun activities, resources, and how to book the author for author visits and events on the website www.tamarahaque.com.au

SCAN ME

Olive Tree Books

www.tamarahaque.com.au